Original title:
Bracelets and Dreams

Copyright © 2025 Creative Arts Management OÜ
All rights reserved.

Author: Seraphina Caldwell
ISBN HARDBACK: 978-1-80586-010-5
ISBN PAPERBACK: 978-1-80586-482-0

Celestial Crafts

In the sky of shiny things,
Where wishes twirl and zing,
A unicorn's spaghetti hat,
Makes people laugh like a silly cat.

Oh, the stars jump around with glee,
Play hopscotch on the moon, you see!
With glittery socks on their toes,
They ride comets like circus pros.

Glint of Ambitions

A jester juggling dreams so bright,
Stumbles on a kite mid-flight,
Each ambition, a bouncing ball,
That giggles as it starts to fall.

Glimmers dance on cheeky grins,
While spaghetti strands appear like fins,
Twirling in a saucy whirl,
Dreams take off, watch them twirl!

Crafted Continuum

A rainbow made of silly strings,
Every color laughs and sings,
Looping dreams like bows so wide,
Pants of polka dots, nothing to hide.

Bubbles float and giggle loud,
In the dreams up in the cloud,
They wear hats of puffed-up air,
With wobbly shoes, without a care.

The Alchemy of Adornment

In a land of chocolate frogs,
Where fables dance like playful dogs,
A wizard makes a magic brew,
With sparkles and laughter, just for you.

Glittering crowns on every head,
Made of marshmallows, never dread,
Each twinkling laugh, a treasure found,
In this world where joy abounds.

Tied Together

Wrist ornaments that jingle and jive,
Each twist and turn, oh how they thrive!
They tell tales of lost socks and stray cats,
Adventures that start with rumbling chitchats.

Bouncing off walls like bouncy balls,
Dancing in circles at neighborhood halls,
Every clasp a hug, every charm a grin,
In this wacky world, we always win!

Echoed Aspirations

Golden glimmers under the sun's gaze,
A mishmash of wishes tangled in a maze,
Frogs in tiaras and ducks with flair,
Silly dreams flutter like butterflies in air.

Each sparkle shouts ambitions quite absurd,
Like llamas in space spilling thoughts unheard,
With magic markers drawing skies of green,
Together we giggle, if you know what I mean!

The Artistry of Affection

Crafted with care like a sandwich divine,
Spread love like butter across toasts we dine,
Bling that brings giggles and questionable sights,
It's art brewed from laughter and silly delights.

Charm a strange llama, dress him in beads,
His fashion sense grows based on friendship needs,
With each little trinket, we build and we share,
A masterpiece formed in colourful flair!

Notes of Nostalgia

Jingly jangly reminders of days gone by,
The ice cream truck playing our favorite cry,
Each shine a story, each bang a cheer,
The laughter of childhood rings crystal clear.

Silly doodles of clowns on a cloud,
Bringing back memories, oh so loud!
With whispers of past, we flash silly grins,
In a circus of life where the chuckle begins.

The Magic of Material

In a world full of glitter, much brighter than gold,
Strings of laughter and stories are eagerly told.
Tangled in colors, they dance on our wrists,
A band of silly moments, who could resist?

A twist here, a twirl there, they jingle with glee,
Each clasp and charm whispers, 'Come laugh with me!'
With each clink and clatter, hopes ride the waves,
As we wear all our wishes like superheroes' capes.

Interlaced Journeys

Travel the trails of whimsical tales,
Where every twist and turn giggles and wails.
With strands intertwined, adventures do grow,
Like a wobbly dance, we put on a show.

Watch out for the tangles, a humorous plight,
As we giggle and stumble from morning to night.
In the realm of connections, each knot holds a grin,
As we stroll through the laughter, let the fun begin.

Spirit in Stone

Dancing in rhythm, with rocks fashioned bright,
Each one holds a punchline, a joke in the light.
From sparkly quartz to a cheeky jade,
They jostle for attention in this playful parade.

With faces so silly, they roll off the tongue,
In a chorus of chuckles, their praises are sung.
They sparkle, they shine, like a punchline divine,
In every playful moment, together we twine.

Whimsy in Wear

Strapped on with giggles, and colors so bold,
Each piece tells a story, both silly and old.
From rubbery bangles to beads made of cheese,
They tickle our fancies with comedic ease.

The mix and the match brings a smile to our face,
In this carnival of whimsy, there's boundless space.
So let us adorn, with laughter and flair,
A quirky collection, a joy we can share.

Illusions in a Loop

A twist, a twirl, a flashy fling,
The jester juggles bling with zing.
In circles bright, the laughter flows,
Around we spin, as chaos grows.

The charmers dance, their tricks on show,
With every twist, their fortunes grow.
They clasp their whims, so bold, so wild,
Like playful thoughts of a giggling child.

Echoes of Elegance

Adorned in hues that clash and clash,
A pageant of colors, a vibrant splash.
Glittering nonsense on every wrist,
Competing for fun, they can't resist.

Shiny layers like tales of old,
Whispers of giggles in stories told.
In fanciful dreams, they frolic and prance,
Unruly charms lead a silly dance.

Shimmering Pathways Unseen

On routes of sparkles, we skip and slide,
With laughter trailing, we take a ride.
Beneath the sun, in glittering art,
Each quirky trinket plays its part.

A flick of the wrist, a wink, a grin,
The world feels wild, let the tomfoolery begin!
Where each step shines like a playful song,
In whimsical patterns, we all belong.

Mystic Circles of Desire

Whirling around, we chase the shine,
In circles we burst, each giddy line.
With wobbly moves, we strut with flair,
A gaggle of giggles fills the air.

A twist of fate, a flick of chance,
We wade through riddles with a jolly dance.
On whims of mischief, we softly tread,
Where laughter leads, we boldly thread.

Allure of the Unspoken

In a world of shiny trinkets,
Who knew they'd cause a fuss?
I wore three on my wrist and thought,
What's life without a plus?

They jangled as I waved my arm,
Like a symphony of sound.
People laughed, I joined the tune,
Wonders in chaos found.

Cupping coffee, a graceful spill,
Each charm took a quick dive.
When I reached for the sugar,
My wrist became alive!

With props for my grand ballet,
I twirled, a sight to see.
But off they flew, like tiny birds,
Oh, where's my jewelry?

Touchstones of the Future

In a marketplace of laughter,
I spotted a quirky thing.
A band that promised fortune,
Yet it made me want to sing!

It shimmered in the sunlight,
Calling me with such delight.
With every twinkle, it seemed to say,
'Join the silly parade tonight!'

I wore it to a fancy ball,
And tripped right on my lace.
The guests erupted into giggles,
Oh, what an awkward grace!

With every twist and every turn,
My outfit turned into a clown.
But joy isn't found in perfect fits,
Sometimes it wears a frown!

Orchestrating Visions in Gold

On my wrist, a tiny orchestra,
Each piece a buzz of sound.
I waved, and suddenly they played,
A tune so profound!

A trumpet charm, a tambourine,
All danced with a joyful clang.
But when I raised my hand up high,
It seemed my wrist just sang!

The chef, he heard the merry chime,
And dropped his ladle down.
Pasta flew like swirling notes,
It became a noodle gown!

I laughed amidst the chaos,
As spaghetti danced around.
With music in the air, I thought,
Life's silliness is profound!

Silken Threads of Intention

A colorful strand around my wrist,
It whispered, 'You'll be bold!'
Yet every time I fidgeted,
Truths about me were told.

One tug and tales unraveled,
About that time I tried to cook.
The smoke alarm was my chorus,
As I burned a favorite book!

I wore it to impress the crowd,
What wisdom did it bear?
But every nod and sideways glance,
Led to some wild stare.

With every loop and knot of fate,
It told of my great mess.
So now I wear it proudly,
A badge of silliness!

Woven Whispers of Wonder

In a mix of colors, my tale does twine,
Dancing in circles, a friend of mine.
It jangles and jests when I go for a run,
Feels like a party, oh what silly fun!

With every slip, it gives a small cheer,
A companion in mischief, always near.
In the sun it glimmers, a shimmer of delight,
Creating laughter, morning 'til night.

Adornments of the Night

Under the glow of the moon's soft beams,
It glows with whispers, it sparkles with dreams.
Each twist and turn tells a story quite neat,
Of a runaway cat and her wild little feats.

When I trip on my shoelace, it gives a good jig,
Like a wobbly dancer who's just had a swig.
It twirls like a dervish with charm so absurd,
Making my antics a sight to be heard!

Threads of Aspiration

With a loop and a spin, we plan big things,
Sales on high fries, and laughter that sings.
Each bead holds a wish, a silly delight,
For a world full of giggles, from morning to night.

It sways with the breeze, a playful tease,
Catching the whispers of mischievous bees.
In a fashion show, it steals the whole scene,
As I strut with swagger, so silly, yet keen!

Celestial Charms and Wishes

Stars twinkle brightly on a bumpy road,
With a jingle and jangle, my happiness flowed.
Each star's a reminder of wishes I've tossed,
Though some turned to puddles, I never feel lost.

Under the playful sky that laughs at my pace,
It guides my adventure with a wink in its grace.
From coffee spills to little quirky quirks,
We dance through the chaos, oh what joyful perks!

A Symphony of Starlit Adornments

In a box where sparkles twitch,
My treasures dance and have a glitch.
A cat once tried to wear a pearl,
Said she was ready to conquer the world.

Glitter shines from random finds,
A rubber band here, a bell that chimes.
My grandma's brooch, now stuck to a sock,
Fashion advice? Better to mock!

Shiny things on my tangled hair,
A disco ball caught unaware.
If jewels could laugh, oh what a feast,
With peculiar styles, we'd be a beast!

Cousins giggle, they shake and twirl,
As my wrist becomes a sparkling swirl.
Together we strut, a hilarious show,
Just wait till the universe sees our glow!

The Ties that Bind and Inspire

Once I lost my glittered thread,
The butler claimed he saw it wed.
To a lamppost wearing lace,
A fashionable, odd embrace.

Mom threw a party, with trinkets galore,
But Cousin Joe thought it a chore.
He wore a watch like an old-timey book,
Said the fashion police didn't look!

Wrist ropes tangle, hearts align,
Each knot is a secret, truly divine.
When my uncle wore a sparkly tie,
We laughed so hard, we nearly cried.

Sisters bicker, they pull and tug,
"Your candy charm looks like a bug!"
Yet through the giggles, the bonds we weave,
In silly styles, we still believe.

Mosaic of Memories Captured

An old shoebox holds a story sly,
Of buttons and odd things I can't deny.
Captured moments in bits and scraps,
Like a dreamer lost in silly naps.

A dance party of mismatched flair,
Beads that wiggle with no care.
A turtle keychain turned into a spy,
Claiming it heard my deepest sigh.

My sister's charm, a unicorn's horn,
Worn as a crown—oh, how we'd scorn!
A charm bracelet on a sleeping cat,
Who knew such joy in such a spat?

Memories strung like colorful lights,
Through silly tales and joyful fights.
Each piece a giggle, a wink, a cheer,
In this mosaic, we hold our dear!

Chapters in a Glimmering Tale

Once there was a page of glittery glee,
Where cosmic doodles danced so free.
Each line a promise and a jest,
Reading it twice makes my heart jest.

I wore a fairy's whimsical crown,
While purple polka dots spun around.
My pen turned into a spicy brush,
Painting laughter, waving a hush.

In this odd tale, my laughter grows,
With surprises tied in every prose.
Each page a treasure, a twisty ride,
As stories and chuckles collide side by side.

We share our quirks with perfect grace,
Adorned in laughter, we find our place.
Together we weave this glimmering shtick,
In chapters of smiles, we giggle and click!

Tangled Inspirations

A twist of fate, a swirl of land,
My wrist is caught, you're not my hand.
Colors clash in a furious dance,
As beads conspire, denied their chance.

Oh, the chaos, a knotted spree,
Sparks of laughter, wild and free.
Each string a tale of tangled glee,
Uproarious joy for you and me.

Shimmering Paths

Like shiny rocks on a winding road,
Each step we take, a stories' load.
A sparkle here, a sparkle there,
Who knew bling could lead to flair?

Chasing glimmers in the sun,
With silly grins, we run and run.
Wobbling left and wobbling right,
Gold can be such a silly sight.

Threads of Enchantment

From simple yarn to cosmic thread,
Purls and loops spin tales, instead.
I tripped on fables, oh, what a mess,
   Crafting magic, but in distress.

A tapestry of blunders bright,
Stitched with giggles, pure delight.
Could these charms weave dreams so grand?
In our folly, we will stand.

Harmonies of the Heart

Strings entwine, a merry song,
Dancing notes feel right, not wrong.
With laughter's tune, our bonds align,
A symphony of absurd design.

Oh, swirl and twirl in joyful spree,
Life's a concert; come sing with me.
With every beat, we waddle about,
Creating rhythms worth a shout!

Woven Whispers

In a world where threads entwine,
Colorful knots create a sign,
Worn proudly with a little glee,
Fashioned whispers, just for me.

Every twist tells tales of cheer,
A quirky laugh, a joke sincere,
Adorning wrists with snazzy flair,
Sunny days, no weight to bear.

With a jingle and a twisty spin,
My party vibes are sure to win,
A rainbow swirls with every move,
Oh what a groove! Let us approve!

As we dance and sway around,
These little charms unlock the sound,
Of giggles shared and memories made,
Where fun and laughter won't ever fade.

Beyond the Surface

Beneath the glimmer, stories play,
Each loop a tale that leads astray,
Fanciful charms that make me grin,
While mischief stirs and laughs begin.

Twinkling tales on my wrist do prance,
Whisking me off into the dance,
Wobbly beads, like spaghetti twirled,
In this whimsical, funny world.

Colors clash like pests in flight,
A carnival of pure delight,
With every jingle, hearts will soar,
Who knew such joy lived at my door?

A lighthearted touch, a playful tease,
As friends all chime with love and ease,
From every corner, joy will surge,
Who knew such fun could so emerge?

Finery of Fantasies

Bedecked in oddities, what a sight,
Jesting gems that dance in light,
Each sparkle a giggle, and oh, what flair,
These tiny treasures start to share.

A cheeky twist, a wink, a grin,
My playful heart begins to spin,
With each quirk wrapped snug and tight,
I wear my joy, it fits just right.

From fairytale whims to silly scenes,
My wrist, a gallery of dreams,
Fanciful wonders that seem to gleam,
In this zany life, I reign supreme.

So let the laughter take the lead,
With each piece, find joy indeed,
As fantasies twinkle, bright but sly,
In this crazy world, we laugh and fly!

Marked by Moments

Jingling memories, here we go,
Tiny reminders of fun in tow,
With every click, the laughter springs,
Funny fables that the wrist brings.

Days filled with giggles, nights full of play,
These trinkets track the fun along the way,
Adventurous buddies each have a say,
In this lighthearted life, come what may!

Snappy stories in colors bright,
Shimmering tales that ignite delight,
Breaking the monotony, one jive at a time,
Together we frolic, mismatched and prime!

As joy wraps around with every swirl,
These quirky bits make hearts twirl,
So here's to the moments, funny and sweet,
In this playful dance, life's a treat!

Traces of Stardust

I found a bunch of shiny things,
They jingle and they dance, like wings.
Adorn my wrist with laughter's grace,
While daydreams flash in a sparkly race.

Oh, one fell off and rolled away,
It made a run for it, of course, hooray!
A tiny thief on its own little quest,
Who knew my charm could be so blessed?

The cat just stares, perplexed and proud,
As I chase my treasures, laughter loud.
What magic lies in these shiny chains,
A circus act runs through my veins!

A squirrel stops to give a cheer,
For all the wonders that appear.
With giggles caught in a rainbow's twist,
Let's chase the sparkles, we cannot resist!

Linked Fantasies

I wear my hopes like shiny rings,
They tiptoe lightly and do silly things.
Link by link, they twist and twirl,
A dance-off down the street, oh what a whirl!

One locket sings a tune so sweet,
While another sneezes—what a treat!
How whimsical these trinkets can be,
Turning life into a comedy spree!

A squawking bird joins in the fun,
With a wink and a quirk, it's never done.
Every charm a tale, some wild, some tame,
Each jingle brings mischief, a sense of acclaim.

So off we go, a curious crew,
With laughter echoing, chasing the blue.
The laughter blooms under sunshine's glow,
In a world of giggles, we steal the show!

Adorning the Mind

Oh, what a sight when the sun hits great,
Bits of color in a magical state.
I wear these wonders with flair and cheer,
Each piece a thought, each thought a sidestep here.

A twinkle here, a twist of fate,
Where laughter blooms, we congregate.
Sparkly whispers dance in the air,
Like lively bubbles, nothing can compare!

I tell my stories with a flourish bold,
These flickering thoughts are prized and told.
Jigs and jiggles, the humor flows,
Like a playful kitten, each moment glows.

In this world of quirks and shining plays,
I'll twirl and spin in a vibrant daze.
For when I shine with each thought unconfined,
Life's a bajillion laughs, unaligned!

The Wearer's Tale

Once upon a wrist, so lively and bright,
Shiny things came to life at night.
They whispered, giggled, rolled and spun,
Creating antics that just can't be done!

In a world of clinks, giggles flew free,
With every twirl, oh, how I'd decree!
A tap dance here, a shimmy there,
My shiny ensemble showed flair beyond compare.

I met a frog who claimed to be grand,
With a crown of jewels, he took my hand.
We leapt and skipped in a wacky parade,
Who knew such moments could be so played?

And as I prance down this fun-filled lane,
Each shimmer and shine drives me insane.
With a wink and a toss, we dance all night,
The wearer's tale wrapped in pure delight!

Elegy of Enchanted Ornaments

In a drawer where trinkets dwell,
The charms converse and giggle well.
They whisper tales of lost romance,
And dream of fate with every chance.

One sparkly star, with a cosmic grin,
Claims that it knows the places I've been.
With every jingle, it tells a joke,
While my old watch just grumps and chokes.

Oh, the stories from an emerald hue,
Of a cat who danced, and a dog who flew!
Why don't these treasures ever learn?
To stop their seating, it's my turn!

As I dust each piece with gentle care,
I swear that one winks beyond compare.
To the rhythm of laughter and cheer,
They remind me: life is better with gear!

Fantasies in a Looping Chain

In a world where goldfish wear bow ties,
And turtles plot their midnight flies.
A loop of charms sings sweet refrains,
While glitter bounces on window panes.

The parrot thinks it's quite the catch,
As rad gems shimmer, they dance and hatch.
In this funny mix, we lose the frown,
While silly beads just swirl around.

A bracelet scored a selfie spree,
Claiming it's living wild and free.
But every snap breaks its clasp,
"Oh no!" it cries, "What a silly gasp!"

And thus the charms unite in jest,
On a quest to become the best.
In a looping chain, oh what a sight,
We laugh and twinkle into the night!

Radiant Cuffs of Possibility

Radiant cuffs hug wrists so tight,
We giggle at how they feel just right.
Each clasp a promise, a funny pact,
For an adventure, what a bold act!

In silver wraps and colors aflame,
A mismatched set, but who's to blame?
The moon's a friend, the sun's a guide,
As laughter echoes where joy resides.

A rubber duck transforms with grace,
Declaring, "This is my happy place!"
With every squeeze, a chuckle bursts,
In this riot of color, the joy is immersed.

So here's to cuffs that dance and jive,
In a world where we feel alive.
With each little wiggle, we chase the balm,
In moments that find us merry and calm!

Secrets Nestled in Silver

A silver box where secrets dwell,
With giggles hidden, all is swell.
Each tiny key unlocks the fun,
In a treasure trove when day is done.

Curly cues and pearls in a spin,
They say mischief starts with a grin.
"What's that?" asks one in quiet awe,
As another shouts, "Let's break the law!"

Wishes scurry like mice, you'd see,
In this shiny nook, all wild and free.
They scheme of pranks and silly plays,
Under the twinkling starlit rays.

So gather 'round, all ye who jest,
In silver whispers, we're truly blessed.
These secrets live, never to part,
In this glittering realm, we share our heart!

Hope's Ornamented Voyage

On a boat made of bling, they set sail,
Laughing like kids, telling wild tales.
Each charm a secret, a giggle, a grin,
Floating through waves, where dreams begin.

With trinkets in hand, they dodge a big wave,
Like pirates of laughter, so utterly brave.
The horizon sparkles, as sunlight does gleam,
They dance on their boat, living the dream.

A pendant of jellybeans, why not?
Wonders of nonsense, so crazy, so hot.
With each goofy smile and a silly cheer,
Their voyage of hope is perfectly clear.

As they reach the shore, they wear crowns of clay,
With laughter in piles, they jump and they play.
Adventures are treasures, on waves they will ride,
Together forever, their joy the true guide.

The Dance of Eternal Keepsakes.

In a room full of laughter, they twirl with flair,
Each keepsake a dance partner, beyond compare.
A bobblehead bobbing, a spoon doing spins,
Clattering together, where the fun begins.

With a wink and a jig, the marbles roll free,
Like confetti, they burst, in sweet jubilee.
What's that in the corner? A rubbery shoe!
Join in the conga, it dances too!

A necklace of noodles, they wear with great pride,
As giggles and wobbling become their new guide.
Flipping and flopping, all joy without cares,
In a funky parade, they dance down the stairs.

The keepsakes keep laughing, as silly as can,
With a goofy old potato, becoming their fan.
From trinket to trinket, they hop and they sway,
In this dance of pure joy, they will forever play.

Adorned Wishes

With buttons and beads strung on yarn,
They dream of a world where unicorns prance.
Each twinkle a giggle, a flutter so bright,
Wishes take flight, like birds in the night.

A bow made of candy, glued on with flair,
Each wish comes alive when spun through the air.
They toss them up high, with giggles so loud,
Watching them soar, feeling ever so proud.

A ring of silly putty, ripe with delight,
Bouncing like bunnies, they giggle at height.
Whispers of whimsy, with every dream sown,
Colorful laughter, in this land they have grown.

Under the moon, they chuckle and sway,
Adorned in their wishes, they dance all the way.
With each bounce and leap, futures seem bright,
In this jolly parade, they bask in the light.

Echoes of Elegance

In a quirky old shop, the echoes resound,
Where elegance tzip zap, spins round and around.
With teacups on their heads, they're feeling quite grand,
Each laugh is a memory, like grains of sand.

A crystal ball bouncing, full of pure glee,
Spin it on fingers, just wait and see!
With laughter like music, it fills up the room,
Where echoes of elegance banish all gloom.

They swan dive in style, with socks polished bright,
As mirrors reflect every whimsical flight.
Draped in bright streamers, with sparkles and cheer,
Each echo of laughter is music to hear.

Through the shelves they glide, with ease and with grace,
Each treasure a ticket to a magical place.
In a whirl of pure joy, they twist and they spin,
Echoes of elegance, where the fun will begin.

Artful Annulments

With twinkle toes and carefree cheer,
A jester's ring flips high in the air.
It dances and prances, a wild bazaar,
While we giggle and chase all our silly dreams there.

A wink from a friend on this fashion spree,
Mismatched wonders, oh what a sight!
Tangled detours in a vibrant spree,
Like knitting with string in the glow of twilight.

Frogs in tuxedos are how we declare,
That laughter's the ticket to secrets we share.
Silly ambitions, just floating around,
Oh, the joy in absurdities we've found!

A feast of confetti, so sparkly and bright,
We snatch at our fancies, oh what a delight!
In the gallery of whimsy we spin like a whirl,
Each twinkling trinket, a giggle unfurled!

The Spell of Debonair

A dapper chap in a polka dot tie,
Claims he can charm both the sun and the sky.
His magic works only on clothes worn askew,
With a wink and a twirl, what more can he do?

He juggles the lemons while calling for fate,
Sips tea with squirrels, oh isn't that great?
Fashion faux pas? Not in his domain,
For the quirkiest trends flow like a runaway train.

Their samba of laughter, an extravagant dance,
All dressed in bits that would put you in trance.
An ensemble he sported, so loud and so proud,
Even pigeons cooed, they were part of the crowd!

And when the moon rises with sparkles galore,
He tiptoes through puddles, leaving us wanting more.
Sassy shenanigans, all under the stars,
With a sprinkle of magic, he'll journey afar!

Tidal Inspirations

Waves crash with laughter on whimsical shores,
Where seaweed becomes crowns for silly explorers.
Flip-flops can sing, if you listen just right,
As crabs throw confetti in merriment bright.

A sunburned seagull strumming a tune,
Squawking wild serenades under the moon.
With shells as guitars, oh the joy we would find,
In surfboard shenanigans, both silly and blind.

Mermaids in flip-flops join in on the fun,
Crafting their dreams as they leap from the run.
A splash here, a honk there, where giggles collide,
It's the ocean of shenanigans, come take a ride!

So let's sail on wobbly boats made of cheese,
With giggles and bubbles dancing on the breeze.
For tides hold the secrets to silliness shared,
With saltwater laughter, our spirits bared!

Hues of Hope

In a world painted lavish in tones so bizarre,
The painter is a monkey with a wand and a car.
He dips in the colors of tickles and glee,
Creating a mishmash like you've never seen!

With crayons as swords, they conquer the night,
A canvas of giggles, an unusual sight.
Every stroke is a jest, a riddle or pun,
Even dogs in top hats join in on the fun!

Pastels in the sky turn the mundane to bright,
As dolphins wear berets in the new morning light.
From laughter in gardens, each blossom's a cheer,
Painting joy with the whimsies we hold ever dear.

In the gallery of dreams, a raucous fair,
Colors embrace us with scents in the air.
Reality shatters, dreams start to blend,
Where laughter and stories dance hand in hand till the end!

Gleaming Pathways

On my wrist, a shiny thing,
It jingles loud when I try to sing.
The cat looks up with a curious eye,
As I dance around, oh me, oh my!

Each glimmer shines, a tiny star,
I laugh so hard, I won't get far.
The neighbor's dog barks in delight,
As I twirl and sprout wings for flight!

But with a slip, I trip on air,
My precious jewels fly everywhere!
I catch them quick, a graceful sweep,
A moment of clumsiness, well, not deep!

In my dreams, I'm a disco ball,
Spinning glitter that makes me tall.
I leap and bound, so free and wild,
With every twinkle, I feel like a child!

Fragments of the Future

I wore a charm of purple hue,
Thinking of all the things I'd do.
I'd fly to Mars on a whim of fun,
With my lucky trinkets, I just might run!

A sparkly piece, so bright and bold,
Told me secrets yet to unfold.
"Go find a unicorn," it did say,
But I ended up in a café today!

I sipped some tea and shot the breeze,
With no horned beasts, just near-sighted bees.
My charm just giggled, a mischievous tease,
As I pondered life, with laughter, I freeze!

The future's fragments, I wear with pride,
A bit silly, but fun's the ride.
I'll flip the world upside down,
Then wear my sparkles as a crown!

Threads of Intuition

A bracelet made of silly strings,
Taught me more than fancy things.
It whispered tales in colors bright,
"Ditch the plans, just take flight!"

I walked the street with my flair on fire,
Chased a pigeon, felt quite the desire.
It led me down paths I've never known,
Where giggling flowers have brightly grown!

In gardens where the laughter flows,
My charm caressed where the wild breeze blows.
"Follow me," it winked with glee,
Towards cookies baked under sunshine's spree!

So I danced with joy, and twirled about,
In a world that spun with cheerful shout.
With threads of magic wrapping tight,
Every whim became pure delight!

Spheres of Serenity

Rolling orbs and twisted tales,
In every nook, adventure prevails.
I slipped one on, it rolled away,
Taking me on a laughable way!

It bounced through puddles, splashed my shoes,
In a game of tag with nothing to lose.
The sun high up, I chased it down,
With every giggle, I'd wear a crown!

It whispered secrets of joyous play,
"Don't take life too seriously today!"
So I took a leap, let laughter soar,
And found pure silliness at my door.

With rolling spheres that hug my wrist,
I embrace my whims, can't resist.
In this lighthearted dance, I can see,
Every chuckle sets my spirit free!

Jewels from the Imagination

In a world where things can shine,
A jar of wishes, oh so fine.
Giggles slip through sapphire beams,
As we dance through silver dreams.

Cakes that twinkle, ice cream glow,
Wonders crafted, just for show.
Lollipop trees in bubble streams,
All are tied to our bright dreams.

A butterfly with sequined wings,
Sipping nectar, joy it brings.
With every laugh, our treasures grow,
Fanciful thoughts, a playful show.

So let's giggle and make a pact,
In this land of light and act,
With winds of joy that never tire,
Our hearts adorned, we'll never retire.

Luminous Links to Fate

Chain of laughter, link so bright,
Wobble when we dance at night.
Pizza slices glimmering gold,
Making memories, brave and bold.

Jelly beans and twinkling stars,
Silly faces, chocolate bars.
Join our hands, let's spin around,
In laughter's glow, our dreams abound.

Footsteps echo on this path,
Whimsical tunes of silly math.
Counting wishes with our toes,
Eager giggles, round it goes.

So let's wear our shining hearts,
As we play through life's sweet parts.
With every link a tale we write,
Shimmering joy, a pure delight.

Charmed Horizons of the Soul

In a garden where colors play,
Giggling flowers sway and sway.
Rings of daisies, crowns of cheer,
Each petal holds a whispered year.

A squirrel hoards the shining fun,
While we leap beneath the sun.
Playful winds that tousle hair,
As we twirl in dreams laid bare.

Our souls like kites in joyous flight,
Chasing bubbles, oh so light.
Charmed horizons, painted skies,
In this realm, the laughter ties.

Each twinkling thought a vibrant hue,
We dance and spin, just me and you.
With hearts so pure, and spirits high,
In this wild bliss, we learn to fly.

Bound by Dreams

Giggles gather in a line,
Each a treasure, oh so fine.
A secret pact of laugh and cheer,
Makes the world feel bright and clear.

Whimsical thoughts we tie so tight,
Like candy fluffs that dance in light.
Our silly hopes all intertwine,
Bouncing joy like love divine.

Jumping puddles, splashes gleam,
In our heads, a silly scheme.
We'll build a castle made of fluff,
With giggles strong and smiles enough.

So here we are, bound in fun,
Underneath the wishing sun.
With every chuckle, we embrace,
A world where joy finds its place.

Freed by Stars

Stardust sprinkled on a toast,
Makes us giggle, laugh the most.
With every bite, we soar and glide,
On a rollercoaster joyride.

Peanut butter, jelly spread,
With a wink and silly thread.
Twirling dreams on rainbow beams,
Crafting smiles from kid-like schemes.

In the night where wishes play,
We gallop through the Milky Way.
With laughter as our guiding light,
We twirl and spin, oh what a sight.

So let's burst forth with every star,
Traveling near and traveling far.
For in our hearts, unchained delight,
Is found in dreams that dance with light.

Tethers of Time and Hope

In a world of shiny things,
I lost my left shoe, it sings.
Wrapped around my wrist so tight,
It glows like disco balls at night.

Each jingle whispers tales of yore,
Of fabric soft and colors galore.
The timing's off, but that's okay,
I dance along, come what may.

Odd objects stuck upon my arm,
They swear they mean no harm.
Each spin and twist, a giggle escapes,
Outrageous charms in funny shapes.

So here we are, with laughter bright,
In the whirl of clinks, all feels right.
I wear my stories, quirky and bold,
A collection of thoughts, more precious than gold.

Emblems of the Heart

Floppy disks and shiny fobs,
A quirky way to solve my snobs.
Each piece, an emblem of my taste,
A mix of whimsy, never misplaced.

Worn like trophies from a fray,
They dance along in their own ballet.
A tiny squirrel and a rubber duck,
Who knew my wrist could hold such luck?

Colors pop like candy shops,
With every clink, I giggle and hop.
Friends ask, 'What's with that glare?'
I just shrug with a silly stare.

So join my jest, come take a glance,
At this wild, whimsical, playful dance.
Where laughter chimes and fun takes flight,
In this adventure, all feels right.

Spheres of Light and Longing

I've got a orb from when I tripped,
At the fair, while my fancy slipped.
Now it sparkles and rolls with glee,
Reminds me of that hotdog spree.

Within this circle of glittering cheer,
The night is young, the end is near.
These trinkets toll as clocks unwind,
Forward I dream, leave past behind.

A yo-yo and bottle cap,
These playful items, a funny chap.
They hum and buzz with tales untold,
Adventures shared and laughter bold.

This sphere of light, a hidden dream,
Visible only in a giggle's beam.
So here's to joy that never fades,
In this merry life, madness cascades.

Trinkets of Tomorrow's Voyage

A paperclip from an old school plan,
And bracelet bits from my brave aunt Jan.
Every piece a map through maze,
Leading me to tomorrow's gaze.

Each bobble jostles with delight,
As I embark on flights of flight.
Hold on tight, wear this charm,
It's my ticket, it can't do harm!

Giggling softly in the breeze,
These trinkets help me, oh, with ease!
A jellybean and a rubber star,
In my heart, they'll go far.

So cheer me on, oh silly strands,
Join me in this world unplanned.
A voyage full of laughter's embrace,
With each trinket, a silly chase.

Unfolding Stories

In a drawer, they jingle and jive,
Adventures await, come take a dive.
Each trinket with tales, from far and wide,
Whispers of laughter that never hide.

One sparkles bright, claims to know it all,
While another insists it's king at the ball.
A dance party occurs when none are around,
They tell silly secrets, oh, what a sound!

Some argue who's oldest, some boast of their charms,
But take a deep breath, it's all just for laughs.
With twists and turns, they treasure the night,
Creating a circus of pure delight.

At dawn they settle, sleepy from glee,
Resting in silence, as cozy as can be.
Awaiting the moment when people arrive,
For the next silly tales to come alive!

Treasures of Tomorrow

A box full of wonders, what lies inside?
Each little bauble, a colorful ride.
Some spin like tops, others dance and chirp,
While mismatched pairs complain and burp!

One claims to grant wishes, oh what a jest,
While another insists it must be the best.
In this silly trove, no frowns allowed,
Wear them with laughter, wear them with pride!

They slip and slide, under couch and chair,
A scavenger hunt, now that's a fair!
"Catch me if you can!" one giggles and hops,
While friends cheer on from the kitchen tops.

At dusk they regroup, with stories to share,
Each one's a treasure, crafted with care.
Tomorrow brings more, who knows what's in store,
New adventures await, let's explore even more!

Charmed by Time

As the clock ticks by, they shimmy and sway,
Each piece a reminder of silly play.
Some sparkle like stars, others fade into chrome,
Each with a wink, they call out for home.

An owl enameled, claims wise like a sage,
While a disco ball spins, releases its rage.
Caught in their charm, we laugh 'til we cry,
Crafting new moments, as time wanders by.

In a pinch, a mishap, one takes a wrong turn,
"Oh no!" they all shout, as they twist and churn.
With giggles aplenty, they dance on the floor,
Creating a ruckus, who could ask for more?

With silver and gold, they lighten the load,
Adorning our lives, on this wacky road.
All in good fun, amid chaos and cheer,
Their charm is eternal, they'll always be here!

Layers of Light

Like an onion's peel, they're stacked with surprise,
Each layer reflecting our goofy lives.
A pop of this color, a dash of that hue,
Together they giggle, as if they all knew.

One layer tells stories, both silly and sweet,
While another makes up rhymes to beat.
In a magical whirl, they twirl 'round the room,
Creating a ruckus, as laughter does bloom.

With shades of the rainbow, a zesty affair,
All come together, no need for a care.
"Always be happy!" the boldest one sings,
And into the night, joyfully they spring.

In layers they linger, through giggles and cheer,
With friendship and laughter, they keep drawing near.
With the flick of a wrist, they shine ever bright,
Creating a canvas of whimsical light!

Captured Light

In a world of shiny things,
Where laughter often rings,
A shimmer caught on playful hands,
Whispers of far-off lands.

With colors bright like jelly beans,
They dance and spin, like tiny dreams,
Each clasp a giggle or a wink,
That makes us stop and think.

In a twist, they start to glow,
As silly as a circus show,
They jingle with a joyful sound,
Where goofiness is always found.

So wear them high, and wear them low,
A treasure chest of fun to show,
In crazy styles, an artful play,
Capturing light in a whimsical way.

Circles of Aspirations

Round and round, the tales we tell,
Like ovals bouncing, cast a spell,
Each circle holds a laugh or cheer,
Spinning dreams that feel so near.

A spiral dance of hopes so bright,
Like spinning tops that take to flight,
Each loop a giggle, each arc a gleam,
In this carnival of scheme.

We gather 'round with smiles and glee,
Juggling wishes, just you and me,
With every twist, the joy expands,
A hoot and holler as life unplands.

So let us twirl through every scene,
In circles sewn with threads of green,
A frolic, a frolic, oh what a life,
In these loops, we thrive, free of strife.

Ties of Serenity

With threads of laughter, brightly spun,
We tie our joys, oh what fun!
In knots of humor, they entwine,
As we giggle and sip our wine.

Each knot a bond, a story shared,
Of silly moments, all prepared,
A loop of peace and playful lore,
Unraveling happiness, wanting more.

Sometimes tangled, often free,
In cozy corners, just you and me,
These ties bring joy, so fresh and bright,
Creating calm from sheer delight.

So let us dance on ties of cheer,
With every laugh, our path is clear,
In serenity's embrace we sway,
Crafting moments from the fray.

Mystical Charms

Once upon a giggle, we found,
Little charms that twirled around,
With secrets whispered, oh so sly,
Like wise old owls who love to fly.

Each charm a riddle, a twist of fate,
That beckons forth to celebrate,
A tale of joy with every gleam,
In this enchanted, playful dream.

They jingle soft like muffled sounds,
Bringing smiles in leaps and bounds,
With every sway, they grant a wish,
Or sprout a giggle — oh how delish!

So gather 'round these wonders rare,
Sprinkling laughter in the air,
In every charm, a sprinkle of fun,
Mystical joy for everyone.

Chains of Potent Whispers

On my wrist, a jingling song,
Telling secrets, all day long.
A twist of fate, a snap, a clap,
It falls off—oh, what a mishap!

Each link a story, or a joke,
In the office, a silent poke.
With every laugh, I lose a chain,
Yet somehow I keep it sane!

A funky charm from a thrift store,
Dressed like a disco dance floor.
It wobbles when I wave hello,
And everyone wants to know!

Clinking tales of past adventures,
Each metal gleams with wild censures.
Every time I twirl my wrist,
I'm lost in laughter, can't resist!

Beads of Tomorrow

In a jar, they bounce and roll,
Each one a dream, with a quirky role.
A couple yell "pick me!" with glee,
While others just sigh, "let us be!"

I strung them up, or so I thought,
But one escapist oversought.
It popped right off, what a surprise,
Now they're scattered, oh what a guise!

Colorful hopes, some chips and cracks,
They giggle as they tumble back.
A wild race across the floor,
Who knew dreams could roll and soar?

Beer bottle tops join this parade,
"Who invited you?" the beads all played.
A necklace formed, a funny sight,
In this chaos, oh what delight!

Threads of Hope

Stitch by stitch, they weave and play,
A gala formed from night to day.
With every twirl, they dance anew,
What silly games, these threads pursue!

One bright hue said, "I'm the star!"
While others claimed, "We'll take it far!"
Twists and knots form friendships tight,
Until they slip, oh what a sight!

The fabric laughs with every tug,
In this world, it's a big hug.
Misfits blend in colorful threads,
They dream aloud, in punchy spreads!

If one unravels, it starts a show,
Unplanned chaos, now watch it go.
Silly patterns spin around,
In this weave, joy can be found!

Gemstone Journeys

Tiny gems with stories bright,
Like little stars, they dance in light.
They roll around, and choo-choo train,
On a journey, never plain!

One says, "I'm the luckiest!"
While another puffs, "I'm the best!"
Rough edges here, a polished flair,
Together weaving dreams to share!

They trip and tumble, oh what fun,
Chasing rainbows, and yes, they run.
With giggles echoing like a bell,
These jewels have tales they're itching to tell!

Together bound, a patchwork crew,
In mishaps found, they start anew.
For every sparkle hides a glitch,
In gemstones' laughter, life's a pitch!

Reflections in Silver

In a shop where shiny things gleam,
A knickknack whispers, "Join my dream!"
With every twist, a giggle escapes,
As we dance in loops, like silly shapes.

A silver band with charms that jingle,
Tells tales of fun where laughter mingles.
They tell me stories of socks and cheese,
And how the world spun with a sneeze!

Around my wrist, a tale is spun,
Of awkward hugs and a three-legged run.
With every twist and every turn,
My heart chuckles, my cheeks still burn.

In a world that sparkles and gleams,
Forget the woes, it's filled with schemes!
With every glance, I'm off the ground,
Wings made of laughter, joy unbound.

Elixirs of Memory

Chasing giggles in a pot of gold,
Each shiny token a story is told.
A pop of color, a splash of cheer,
Goes hand in hand with a slice of beer!

Here lies a charm of spaghetti and sauce,
It brings to mind that silly toss!
With every trinket, oh how we prance,
In leaps of folly, we take our chance.

One twist of a loop, a blush on my face,
Reminds me of times in a crowded place.
The laughter shared, the silly blunders,
Floating like balloons up into the wonders.

A memory brewed, all sparkly and bright,
It glows in the dark like we own the night.
Each piece is a wink, a bright little spark,
In a world so wild, we'll leave our mark.

Crafting Tomorrow

With crafts and clinks, we weave our plans,
A jester's hat, oh how it spans!
A ticking clock, we dance and twirl,
Each stroke of joy makes our heads swirl.

Crafting futures with silly schemes,
Dreams bubble up like fizzy creams.
A splash of paint, a sprinkle of fun,
Laughter echoes, the day's begun!

Every bead a promise, a laughter thread,
In the chaos of life, where silliness tread.
As we stitch the hours, we chuckle and cheer,
For tomorrow shines bright when friends are near.

With humor we craft, we make it right,
In a workshop where giggles ignite.
Every turn and twist, a chance to stand,
In our whimsical world, our dreams are grand.

Whispers of Possibility

In the garden of whimsy, we dig with delight,
Pots of sunshine and colorful light.
Each shiny token, a wish in disguise,
Reminds us that joy comes in surprise.

Dancing with shadows, we bop and sway,
With whispers of dreams that lead us astray.
Each flick of the wrist, a new path unfolds,
In mystery laughter, life's story is told.

Glimmers of chance, we chase with a smile,
Navigating mishaps with the goofiest style.
Each step we take, echoes leaping around,
With pockets of joy we've happily found.

So let's prance in circles, make merry and cheer,
In our magical world, there's nothing to fear.
With every twinkle, our spirits ignite,
In a dance of possibility, everything's bright!

Adorned Horizons

An outfit can be dull, like a rainy day,
But sparkles make it dance, in a cheeky way.
With a jingle and a wiggle, we make it bold,
As laughter's in the air, and stories unfold.

Wear a little shine, don't be shy or meek,
Jovial bling blings, in shades of unique.
Like candy-coated rainbows, oh what a sight,
They cheerfully wink in the warm sunlight.

Clinks bring some giggles, in the busiest streets,
Fashion giants laughing, at their own silly feats.
Chasing after dreams, in a playful embrace,
With every shiny bit, we quicken our pace.

A wardrobe party, come join in the fun,
With flair on our arms, the night has begun.
Dancing through life, let's make memories,
With a wink and a laugh, as bright as the seas.

Harmonized Whispers

Jangles that chatter, like curious birds,
Chatting away, without needing words.
Each piece a story, our arms have conspired,
To rouse all the giggles that we so desired.

Twirling and spinning, oh what a sight,
As colors collide in playful delight.
With laughter cascading, our worries take flight,
Tiny jingles echo, into the night.

Mix and match madness, no rules to obey,
We drape on the nonsense, hip hip hooray!
Smiles stretch wide, with every new layer,
Who knew fashion fun could be such a player?

So strut down the path, with whimsy and flair,
Each sound leads the way, oh, do you dare?
Wearing our joy, like badges of glee,
In this world we create, forever carefree.

Fragments of Faith

Tiny charms, like secrets, they giggle and sway,
As we march through the garden of our wildest play.
Each blink a reminder of whimsy and light,
Keeping dreams alive, as we dance through the night.

Mismatched treasures, in all shades and hues,
Converse like magpies, trading quirky views.
With a clatter and a clash, their conversations flow,
In the carnival of style, our wishes will grow.

Tales wrapped around our arms, they whisper and tease,
As we skip through the chaos of time's gentle breeze.
Each glittering promise, a giggle unbound,
In this jolly domain, our hearts dance around.

So let's don our laughter, let our spirits rise,
With every little chime bringing joy to our eyes.
The fragments of wonder, we proudly embrace,
In every silly twinkle, we've found our own place.

The Poetry of Adornment

In a world of patterns, let's funk up the scene,
With shiny distractions, quite raucous and keen.
Wearing joy like a badge, oh, isn't it grand?
With a click and a clack, we together will stand.

Each piece a giggle, a twist in the tale,
With bells that chime, we set off like a sail.
Breaking all limits, just say what you feel,
Our whimsical antics, the world will reveal.

Comfy in chaos, our style is a mess,
But laughter is perfect, if you'll just confess.
Wrapped in our whimsy, mischief is born,
Fashioning laughter, with every new morn.

So strut out with flair, don't keep it inside,
With every bright shimmer, let joy be your guide.
In this merry parade, our spirits take flight,
With glittery giggles, we're happy tonight.

Adorned Imagination

In a shop of shiny trinkets,
I lost a sock, but gained a wink.
The laughter wrapped around my wrist,
Now all my thoughts just dance and clink.

With candy colors jangling loud,
I strutted through the market's cheers.
My friends stared, puzzled and amazed,
At my wrist's wild party gears.

Silly things atop my arm,
Like dancing ants in a silly hat.
I twirled and spun with raucous joy,
Who knew a sock could do all that?

So come, let's craft a quirky thread,
Out of giggles and glimmers bright.
We'll wear our quirky joys around,
And turn the mundane into light.

Remnants of Reverie

A dream spilled out in glitter chips,
I gathered them in empty jars.
Now on my wrist, a shining mess,
Looks like I'm friends with shooting stars.

Each bead a tale, a laugh, a sigh,
An ice cream cone, a puppy's bark.
They jangle as I skip on by,
While murmuring, 'This is the spark!'

Swirls of colors, oh what a sight,
A carousel of wondrous bliss.
I trip on thoughts, a humorous ride,
And wonder how I'm missing this.

But oh, these jewels, they make me grin,
Like silly poems that dance and fight.
With every jingle, joy begins,
As laughter wraps me up so tight.

Wistful Charms

A little charm that's just a pig,
Waving hello on my wrist today.
I giggle at his goofy jig,
As he sways and steals my grey away.

Tiny cars, bright bananas too,
All happily racing in place.
They cheer me on, all gleaming new,
In this zany, whimsical space.

When friends ask what I wear with pride,
I smile and giggle on the way.
They'll never guess what's tucked inside,
A world where silliness holds sway.

So let's stack them high, this playful loot,
With each trinket a story to share.
Life's a laugh in this charm-filled suit,
As joy becomes a vibrant flare.

Between the Links

There's magic hiding in my chains,
With each link whispering a rhyme.
A rubber duck, a tiny car,
And one that's shaped like pizza, sublime.

They dance along my wrist, oh please,
A funky parade of thoughts so bright.
I jiggle, jolt, and shimmy with glee,
Proving life's a quirky delight.

With every jangle, a tale unfolds,
Of ice cream cones and silly shoes.
Each charm a ticket—come, behold,
How laughter's just a whim to choose.

So here's to chaos wrapped in joy,
To the wonders found in everyday things.
Let's wear our laughter like a toy,
For each jingle, the pure joy it brings.

The Language of Adornment

With jingles and sparkles, we dance around,
Each shiny trinket, a joke to be found.
A twist here, a loop there, what's this on my wrist?
A charm that just laughs, it can't be missed!

In corners, they giggle, these shiny delights,
Telling me stories of whimsical nights.
You thought it was magic? Just a hug from the bling!
But really, it's just what the whimsy can bring!

Each bead holds a secret, a wacky old tale,
Of dancing with squirrels or riding a whale.
I wear them with pride, these odd little bits,
What can I say? I have strange little wits!

So grab a few baubles, let's frolic and sing,
In this silly parade, it's the laughter we bring.
With every mistake that we might just embrace,
Our adornments remind us, let's hike on with grace!

Interwoven Visions

Tangled in laughter, these loops all collide,
An audience of pixels, all winking with pride.
Who knew such wild colors could get on so well?
In a circus of glitter, stories they tell.

I'm caught in a snare of affection so grand,
A wild little wildflower that slipped from my hand.
Weaving together like a cat in a hat,
A riot of fashion, oh, how about that?

They jingle and jive as I shimmy and shake,
What's that noise? Oh, a whacky earthquake!
Not quite the rhythm of days gone awry,
But certainly laughter that flies through the sky!

Let's twirl in this madness, call it a game,
Each twist and each turn, none of it's lame.
In a world filled with laughter, we're just having fun,
With threads full of quirk, oh, we've just begun!

Sparkling Echoes

A twinkle here, a sparkle there, oh, what do I see?
It's the echoing laughter of a whimsical spree.
Each shine is a giggle caught up in the night,
Bouncing off walls with such gleeful delight.

As I jingle and jangle about in a trance,
You'll not believe the mischief – oh, join in the dance!
With colors exploding like a popsicle burst,
In the game of gaiety, well, who'll quench their thirst?

They dance like they're silly, like they own the whole thing,
While I sit on the sidelines, my heart starts to sing.
With each shiny moment, I can't help but grin,
For in this wild whirl, everyone's sure to win!

Let's skip through this madness, where fun takes the lead,

With echoes of laughter—oh yes, we shall feed!
A feast of pure joy wrapped up in a bow,
In the land of the silly, let's not take it slow!

Glimmers of Tomorrow

Tomorrow looks bright, with a wink and a spin,
Our future's a joke, oh where do we begin?
I've got a collection that's sewn with pure glee,
Dreamy little bits of vibrancy just for me!

With a twist of my wrist, the giggles take flight,
I'll wear my fond memories, oh, what a sight!
A rainbow of wonders, like candy canes pop,
Let's gather 'round, friends, and giggle non-stop!

The hues of tomorrow, they twirl and they prance,
Inviting us all to a fanciful dance.
In the spirit of fun, we'll tickle the time,
For from chaos, we weave a fanciful rhyme!

Here's to the moments where laughter lives free,
No holding back smiles, it's our jubilee!
With a dash of quirkiness, we'll shimmer and sway,
In our delightful parade, let's frolic and play!

www.ingramcontent.com/pod-product-compliance
Lightning Source LLC
Chambersburg PA
CBHW070308120526
44590CB00017B/2592